The Silliest VALENTINE'S DAY JOKE BOOK FOR KIDS AND FAMILY

RIDDLELAND

INTRODUCTION

A Message from Cupid

Hello there, my lovely friend.

Can you feel it? The air is buzzing with excitement, candy hearts are everywhere, and pink and red decorations are popping up all around. That can only mean one thing. Valentine's Day is almost here.

All over the world, people are writing cards, sharing treats, and finding small ways to say, "You matter to me." There are smiles to share, hugs to give, and kind words floating through classrooms, homes, and hearts. But tell me something. Have you practiced your Valentine jokes yet?

If not, you are in luck. Inside this book, you will find hundreds of joyful jokes that are sure to make people smile. There are silly questions, playful puns, and knock knock jokes that might even make me miss my target from laughing too hard.

Each chapter is like a little Valentine surprise, ready to be shared. You will find jokes about candy, cards, Cupid, and all kinds of love filled silliness. The jokes are neatly organized, so whether you need a joke for a class party, a friend, or a family laugh, you can find one in no time at all.

Some jokes are sweet. Some are extra corny. And some are just plain goofy. That is part of the fun. Laughter brings people together, and sharing a joke is one of the easiest ways to spread kindness.

So grab a comfy seat, open to the first chapter, and let the laughter begin. Tell these jokes at school, tuck them into Valentine cards, or surprise someone you love with a smile. Every laugh you share is a little gift.

Remember, Valentine's Day is not only about candy and cards. It is about kindness, joy, and making others feel good. And nothing shows love quite like laughter shared together.

With hugs and happy smiles,
Cupid

TABLE OF CONTENTS

Introduction pg.3

Table of Contents pg.4

Chapter One: Sweet Question-and-Answer
Jokes pg.5
(Quick laughs with a Valentine twist!)
- Loveable Animals pg.7
- Candy Questions pg.10
- Valentine Cards & Notes pg.11
- Cupid's Arrow Antics pg.12
- Blooming Flowers pg.13
- Sweet Treats & Tasty Snacks pg.14
- Hearts & Hugs pg.16
- Random Silly Stuff pg.17
- People, Friends & Funny Feelings pg.23

Chapter Two: Pun-Tastic Valentine Jokes pg.27
(So corny, they're sweet!)
- Animal Puns with Heart pg.29
- Candy Wordplay pg.37
- Silly Card Word Play pg.38
- Cupid-Approved Puns pg.41
- Flower Power Fun pg.42
- Food That's Full of Love pg.43
- Heart-Stopping Humor pg.55
- Objects with a Silly Side pg.56
- Friends and Family pg.78

Chapter Three: Knock-Knock Valentine
Jokes pg.103
(Knock, knock... who loves you?) pg.104

Did You Enjoy The Book? pg.126

About Riddleland pg.127

CHAPTER ONE:
SWEET QUESTION AND ANSWER JOKES

Valentine's Day is full of questions.
The most famous one is, of course, "Will you be my Valentine?"
But that is not the only question people ask this time of year.
Question-and-answer jokes are funny because they surprise you.
Sometimes a word is used in a way you do not expect.

Other times, the answer sounds serious at first, but then turns silly. That little twist is what makes these jokes so fun to tell and even more fun to hear.

In this chapter, you will find Valentine jokes with clever questions and playful answers. Some are goofy. Some are corny. And some might make you laugh before you even finish reading them.

So get ready to ask some funny questions and share some silly replies. Here are a few questions you might hear this Valentine season, along with the jokes you can use to make everyone smile.

What did the teeth ask
the shy dentist on Valentine's Day?

"Do you have fillings for any of us?"

What can you do to alter
a long-standing relationship?

Sit down.

LOVABLE ANIMALS

Why do T. rexes
have short arms?

So they can hold their loved ones close to their hearts.

What did the mammoth
say to his wife?

"I wooly love you."

What did the bay gull call
to the seagull on Valentine's Day?

"Hey, gull friend."

Why were the male moths
so attracted to the lightbulb?

They found her glowing.

What did one lovebird
say to the other?

"Let me call you tweetheart."

**What did the fly
say to his Valentine, the spider?**

"I'm caught in your web!"

**What did one firefly
say to the other?**

"You light up my night."

**What do you
call young fish in love?**

Guppy love.

**What did the bee
call his sweetheart?**

"Honey."

**What did the cow
say to her date?**

"You're udderly amazing!"

**What did the romantic male ladybug
prefer to be known as instead of "ladybug?"**

"The love bug."

What do frogs
say on february 14?

"Hoppy Valentine's Day."

What did the owl
say to his Valentine?'

"Owl always love you!"

CANDY QUESTIONS

Why are the candy store
employees so happy?

The candy store is a sweet place to work.

What did the chocolate bar
say to the candy heart?

"We're a sweet pair."

VALENTINE CARDS & NOTES

What happened when people put their hopes in the mailperson bringing Valentine's greetings?

He delivered.

Why was the Valentine's Day envelope so giddy?

She had romantic feelings inside of her.

How did the chicken farmer get a job writing Valentine's Day greeting cards?

He was great at poultry (poetry) and rhyming words.

CUPID'S ARROW ANTICS

**What's Cupid's
favorite school subject?**

Archery class!

**If Cupid is your foe,
what do you refer to him as?**

Your arch(er)-nemesis.

BLOOMING FLOWERS

What do you call
two florists who are pals?

Buds.

What kind of flowers
should you NOT give on Valentine's Day?

Cauliflowers!

When the Three Musketeers started
their Valentine's flower business, what was their slogan?

"All for one, and one floral."

♥ SWEET TREATS & TASTY SNACKS ♥

**What did the egg
say to the bacon?**

"We're better side by side!"

**What happened when the cookies met
on the cookie sheet, going into the oven?**

It was a batch made in heaven.

**What did the cupcake
say to the frosting?**

"You complete me!"

**What did one coffee
say to the other?**

"I love you a latte."

**What did the bread
say to the jelly on Valentine's Day?**

"I loaf you."

Why did the waffle
fall in love with the syrup?

She was wonderfully sweet!

What did the pizza
tell the pepper?

"You add spice to my life!"

Why was the heart recruited
to be a drummer?

It could keep a beat.

What did the heart whisper
to the shy brain?

"Stop overthinking, just feel!"

RANDOM SILLY STUFF

What did the glue stick
say to the paper?

"I'll never let you go!"

What did the soccer ball
say to the soccer player?

"I get a kick out of you."

What did one garden statue
coo to the other?

"My love for you gnomes no bounds."

What did the Earth
say to the sun on Valentine's Day?

"My world revolves around you."

What did the coloring book
say to the crayon?

"You color my world!"

**What did one hair
say to the other hair on Valentine's Day?**

"I love you unconditionally."

**What did the booger
say to the nose on Valentine's Day?**

"I'm blown away by you."

**What did the compass
say to the map?**

"You give my life direction!"

**What did the cloud whisper
to the sun?**

"You brighten my day."

**What did one sock
say to the other sock?**

"We make a great pair."

**What did the candle
say to the match?**

"Come on, baby; light my fire!"

**What did the puddle
say to the raindrop?**

"You complete me!"

**What did the baseball mitt
say to the baseball?**

"You're quite a catch."

What did the light socket
say to the appliance?

"I love you watts."

What did the pillow
say to the blanket?

"We make a cozy pair, don't we?"

What did one firework
say to the other?

"You light up my night!"

What did the jelly
say to the knife?

"You spread happiness!"

What did the raindrop
say to his Valentine?

"Water you doing tonight?"

What happened to
the romantic snowman?

He melted into his Valentine's arms.

How did the ocean greet
its Valentine?

It waved.

What did the magnet
write on its Valentine's?

"You pull me in."

What did one shoe say to the other?

"We make a great pair!"

What did the soccer ball say to the goal?

"You're the reason I'm here."

Why did 2 break up with 0?

Because some 1 came between them.

What did the camera say to its crush?

"I'm focused on you."

Why did the robot fall in love with the toaster?

Someone had replaced its hard drive with a heart drive.

What did the thumb say to the finger on a cold winter day?

"I'm in glove with you."

How quickly do pilots
give their hearts to stewardesses?

It's often love at first flight.

What did the paratrooper
say to his instructor?

"I'm falling for you."

Why was everyone happy
when the Cyclops married his girlfriend?

They knew he had his eye on her for a long time.

What did the eye doctor
say to his Valentine?

"You're a sight for sore eyes."

Why didn't the comedian
tell any jokes to his girlfriend?

It was a serious relationship.

Why do some people constantly mention St. Patrick and St. Valentine in their conversations?

They like to get their two saints in.

What did the Blob say to his girlfriend on Valentine's Day?

"Will you be my Valen-slime?"

What did the hiker say to his prospective Valentine?

"Where is the trail to your heart?

What does the gardening grandmother like to plant on her grandkids on Valentine's Day?

Kisses.

What happened when the man fell in love with the fry cook who wrote poetry?

He married her for batter or for verse.

What did the pie-maker say to his Valentine?

"I've got fillings for you."

What did the artist
tell his girlfriend?

"I love you with all my art."

What should you do if you promise
your date the moon, sun, and stars?

Take her to a planetarium.

What did the baker
say about being loyal to his Valentine?

"I only have pies for you."

What did the climber
with his broken leg in a cast say to his Valentine?

"I've got a crutch on you."

Why did the mother not want her daughter
to date the magician?

She was afraid he would disappear.

What did the gardener
say to his wife?

"I love you from my head tomatoes."

What's a pirate's favorite thing
to say to his Valentine?

"You ar-r-r-r-r my greatest treasure!"

CHAPTER TWO:

PUN-TASTIC VALENTINE JOKES

Punny jokes are all about words that like to play tricks on your brain. They usually start with a simple question, but the answer means more than one thing. That little surprise is what makes a pun so funny.

Take a joke like, "Where did the two clothespins fall in love?" The answer is "Online." At first, you might think of the internet. But clothespins also hang out on a clothesline. When you realize the answer works both ways, that is when the joke really clicks.

That is the fun of pun jokes. Your brain jumps to one meaning, then suddenly spots another. When both ideas fit at the same time, it feels clever, silly, and satisfying all at once.

In this chapter, you will find Valentine puns that are sweet, corny, and a little bit sneaky. Read them slowly, say them out loud, and watch the smiles appear. The more you share these jokes, the funnier they become.

Now get ready to stretch your brain, twist some words, and laugh along the way. Let the pun fun begin.

Where did the two clothespins
fall in love?

Online.

What did the calculator
say to its Valentine?

"You can count on me."

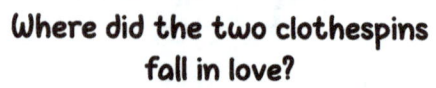

MRC   M+

CE

ON/C   0   .   −   +

What are
the most romantic bugs?

The fruit flies; it seems they are always on dates.

What did the flirting bee
call to the flowers?

"Which one of you wants to be my honey?"

What did one shy fish
say to the other?

"You're being koi."

What did the turtle
say to his Valentine?

"You make me come out of my shell!"

Why did the dog
write a sad love song?

Because he had a ruff life!

What did the bird give
his sweetheart on February 14?

A Valentine's tweet!

What did the elephant
say to her giraffe boyfriend?

"You're head and shoulders above anyone else I've ever met!"

What do you
call a sheep's Valentine?

A love ewe note!

Why did the two flat fish
get along so well?

They were sole mates.

What did the seal say to her current Valentine
when she wanted a new Valentine?

"I think we should see otters."

What did the embarrassed pig
say to her Valentine?

"You're acting like a ham."

**What did the reindeer
say to its Valentine?**

"I caribou you."

**How did the terns know
they were supposed to be together?**

Because one good tern deserves another.

What did the bat
say to his girlfriend?

"Want to hang?"

What form of poetry did the pigeon on the rooftop
use to woo the pigeon on the rooftop next door?

High coo.

How did the shy sheep flirt
with the other sheep?

Sheepishly.

Which animals give
the most hugs?

Bears. Bears like to give bear hugs.

Which fish is
the most romantic?

The one with a sole mate.

What did the young deer
say to his Valentine?

"I'm fawned of you."

Why did the bee visit
the flower on Valentine's Day?

He was searching for his honey.

What did the zebra
say to the whiney, lonely lion on Valentine's Day?

"Don't you have any pride?"

Why did the ram say "yes" with a smile to everything the female sheep told him to do, but was grouchy with everyone else?

Because he only has ayes for ewe.

What did the male sheep
say to his girlfriend?

"There will never be another ewe."

What did the owl whisper
to the other owl?

"You're a hoot!"

Why did the cat
write a card for its Valentine?

To show it was feline fine.

How did people know the frog
was a little nervous at the Valentine's Day dance?

It was a little jumpy!

What time of
the year do bedbugs fall in love?

In the spring.

**What did
the buck coo to the doe?**

"Oh, dee-e-e-e-er?"

**Why did the lioness hug
the lion's furry neck?**

That was her mane squeeze.

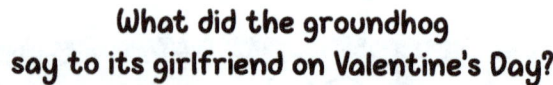

What did the groundhog
say to its girlfriend on Valentine's Day?

"I gopher you."

What did the worm
say to his girlfriend who lived in a cantaloupe?

"You're one in a melon."

What happened
when the squirrel fell in love?

Its life got even nuttier.

What do you call
a Valentine's kiss from a dog?

Puppy love!

CANDY WORDPLAY

What is the airline pilot's
favorite type of candy?

Plane chocolate.

Is most Valentine's candy
used wisely?

No. It goes to waist.

What type of Valentine's candy
do musicians prefer?

Rock.

What part of a Valentine's Day candy bar
is the most musical?

Candy wrapper.

What did the chocolate truffle
say to his Valentine?

"Life is sweet when I'm with you!"

Why did the chocolate bar blush?

Because it saw the candy kiss!

SILLY CARD WORDPLAY

Why don't
most Valentine's Day cards get lonely?

They come in packs.

Why did the Valentine's card
get an "A" at school?

Because it had perfect handwriting - and lots of heart!

What kind of
Valentine's Day cards play music?

Noteworthy ones.

Do letter carriers drive fast?

They drive post haste.

What do informed mail carriers
do on Valentine's Day?

Keep you posted.

What can salesclerks do to enhance Valentine's Day card sales?

Push the envelope.

Which professionals get the least daily exercise?

People who sell Valentine cards tend to be associated with stationery.

Why did the ghost give
Valentine's cards to his friends?

Because he wanted to lift spirits!

Where do letter carriers place
Valentine's Day cards for boys?

In the male box.

Why did the Valentine's Day card envelope
go to the doctor?

It felt stuffed up.

Why was
the Valentine's Day card's envelope wet?

The postage was dew.

What did the postage stamp
say to the envelope on Valentine's Day?

"I'm stuck on you."

What did the envelope
say to the postage stamp?

"Stick with me; we'll go somewhere."

40

CUPID APPROVED PUNS

What happens
when that famous archer Cupid gets nervous?

He quivers.

Why does Cupid
carry a pen in his pocket?

So he can draw a bow.

Why don't more people participate
in archery like Cupid?

Archery has a lot of drawbacks.

What did Cupid, Robin Hood
and William Tell say to their girlfriends?

"Most people think of me as an archer, but I'll gladly be your beau."

Why was Cupid
sharpening his arrows?

He had a point to make.

Why have some people playfully nicknamed
the cherub that shoots arrows "Stupid Cupid"?

They're referring to his errors instead of his arrows.

FLOWERS AND PUNS

How is the letter "A"
similar to a flower?

Both often have a bee come after them.

What did the seed
say to the budding flower?

"You've grown on me!"

Why did the heartbreaker
give his girlfriend a goodbye flower?

He wanted her to have some buddy to love.

What kind of flower
gives the best kisses?

Tulips! (Two lips)

What kind of romance did
the young flowers have?

A budding romance.

What kind of flower did
the squirrel give to his Valentine?

A forget-me-nut.

What did the greenhouse owner
say to his Valentine?

"I will love you today and floral time."

43

♥ FOOD THAT'S FULL OF LOVE ♥

Guess what's going to be spoiled
on Valentine's Day?

The milk dated before February 14.

What did one pancake
say to the other?

"I flip for you!"

Why did the boy whisper,
"Doughnuts, candy, and cake. Doughnuts, candy, and cake?"

He was saying sweet things.

What did the chip
say to the dip?

"We were made for each other."

How did the pumpkin
flirt with the corn?

It whispered in its ear.

44

**What did the lettuce
give its Valentine?**

A piece of its heart.

**What did the cake
say to the ice cream?**

"I think you're cool."

What attracted
the nacho chip to the nacho dip?

She liked cheesiness.

What did the ice cream
say to the hot fudge?

"You make me melt."

What did the plain chicken nugget
say to the spicy chicken nugget on Valentine's Day?

"You're hot!"

What did the coffee
say to the sugar?

"You make my life sweet!"

What happened when the dating woman
had to choose between dessert and her Valentine?

The decision was a piece of cake.

What did the hot dog
say to its Valentine?

"We're in a frank relationship."

Why did the hamburger
go to the barbecue?

He was looking for an old flame.

What did the marshmallow
say to the hot chocolate?

"I melt in your presence."

How did the baker woo his Valentine?

With lots of flours.

Why were monkeys attracted to the banana?

It had appeal.

What did the plain side of the bread say to the side that was buttered?

"You're my butter half."

What did the corn chip say to the cheese on Valentine's Day?

"Together we're nacho average Valentine's couple."

What did the marshmallow say to the flame on Valentine's Day?

"You make me feel gooey inside!"

Why did the tea get so many Valentine's?

It was extra sweet.

What did the margarine
say to the bread when they ended their romance?

"You deserve butter."

How is the romance between sweet tea
and unsweet tea best described?

Pitcher perfect.

**What did the blender
say to the smoothie ingredients on Valentine's Day?**

"I have mixed feelings, but I think we might blend together well."

**Why did the teenage boy
take a fig to the Valentine's Day dance?**

He couldn't find a date.

**What did the coffee bean
say to his Valentine?**

"We're the perfect blend."

**What did the gum wad
say to the shoe on Valentine's Day?**

"I'm stuck on you."

**Which vegetable is known
for being nice?**

The sweet corn.

**What did the coffee-drinker
say to his Valentine?**

"You have a latte heart."

50

**What do you call
a banana that flirts?**

A banana smoothie.

**What did the girl think of
the homemade sugar cookies her Valentine brought her?**

She thought they were very sweet.

**How did the onion propose
to his sweetheart?**

He gave her a ring.

**Why did the orange
fall in love with the banana?**

It has appeal.

**What did the burger
give his Valentine?**

An onion ring.

**What did the pizza
say to its Valentine?**

"You've got a pizza my heart!"

**What did the potato
say to its Valentine?**

"I only have eyes for you."

**What did the banana
say to its Valentine?**

"I love you bunches."

What did the gardener
say to the potato on Valentine's Day?

"I dig you."

Why did the boy bring the girl a low-priced fruit
from a flowering palm tree?

She said she wanted a cheap date.

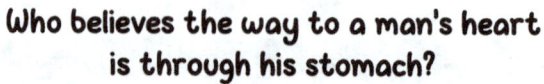

Who believes the way to a man's heart
is through his stomach?

Really bad surgeons.

Passion fruit may be the most romantic fruit;
what is the least romantic fruit?

Peaches; peaches have a heart of stone.

What did one slice of pizza
say to the other slice?

"It may be cheesy, but I love you."

HEART-STOPPING HUMOR

Why did the heart join
the track team?

It liked to race.

Why date
a cardiologist (heart doctor)?

They know how to treat a heart.

What is
the natural color of a heart?

Beat red.

What color is
a broken heart?

A broken heart is very blue.

OBJECTS WITH A SILLY SIDE

What did the reader
say made her fall in love with her dictionary?

"I think my dictionary loves me because its words have meaning."

What did the refrigerator
say to the magnet?

"I find you attractive."

What did the Bluetooth phone
say to the television?

"I think there may be a connection between us."

What did the limestone
say to its girlfriend?

"Don't take me for granite."

What did the boy candle
say to his candle sweetheart?

"I want to go out with you."

Why did
the comic book characters fall in love?

They were drawn together.

What did the laptop
say to the charger on Valentine's Day?

"I'd die without you."

What tree is named in honor of people who long for lost love?

Pine.

What did the paper say to the printer ink on Valentine's Day?

"You are my type."

What did the boy leaf on the tree branch say to the girl leaf on the ground right before he let go of the tree branch?

"I'm falling for you."

Why did the grape stop dating?

It was afraid of getting crushed.

What happened when the microwave and the metal got together and fell in love?

Sparks flew.

What is the most romantic tree?

Maple trees; they are very sappy.

What did the test-tube say to its Valentine?

"We've got great chemistry together."

How did the knife get the roll to pay attention to him on Valentine's Day?

He buttered her up.

Why did the river
fall in love with the spring?

She was bubbly.

How did the red blood cell's courtship of
the white blood cell go?

It was all in vein.

What did the ground
say to the shovel on Valentine's Day?

"You make me whole."

What cruise boats
do Valentines' ride together?

The court ship and friend ship.

What did one shirttail
say to the other on Valentine's Day?

"I like hanging out with you."

What did the land
say to the sea on Valentine's Day?

"I was in love with you ever since you waved."

Why did the math book go to the Valentine's Dance with the multiplication table?

It wanted good times.

Why was the eraser upset with its Valentine?

It felt rubbed the wrong way.

Why did the volcano
get a date?

It was smoking hot!

Why did the snowman
not return the girls' affection?

He had a cold, cold heart.

What did the shy umbrella
say to the rain?

"You make me open up."

What did the refrigerator
say to the freezer?

"You're the coolest."

Why didn't the bike
go to the Valentine's Day dance?

It was too tired.

Why did the skeleton
give candy hearts?

Because it didn't have the guts to say, "I love you."

What did the leaves on the tree say to the wind?

"You blow me away."

Why did the balloon stay home on Valentine's Day?

It didn't want to get carried away!

What did one ghost
say to the other on Valentine's Day?

"You're my boo!"

Why did the tonsil think the doctor
was going to ask it to be its Valentine?

She heard the doctor saying he was going to take her out.

What did the tidepool
say to the other tidepool on Valentine's Day?

"Show me your mussels!"

What happened
when the electrical cords met?

There was a spark between them.

What did the pencil
say to the eraser on Valentine's Day?

"You're just write for me!"

Why did the computer
not want to go on a Valentine's date with the keyboard?

She wasn't his type.

What happened
when the two strands of rope fell in love?

They tied the knot.

Why did the candle fall in love?

It found its perfect match.

**What did the piece of tape
say to the paper on Valentine's Day?**

"I'm stuck on you."

**What did the female raindrop
say to her friends on Valentine's Day?**

"I love my rain beau."

**What did one bowling pin
say to the other bowling pin on Valentine's Day?**

"Let's never split."

**What did one lung
say to the other lung on Valentine's Day?**

"We be-lung together."

**Why didn't the skeleton
ask his girlfriend for a date?**

He didn't have any guts.

**What did the ghost
say to his ghoul-friend on Valentine's Day?**

"I'd walk through fire for you. . . . And walls. I'd walk through walls too."

**What did the cactus coo
to the other cactus?**

"Aren't you looking sharp today?"

**What did the 90-degree angle
say to the other 90-degree angle?**

"I think we're right for each other."

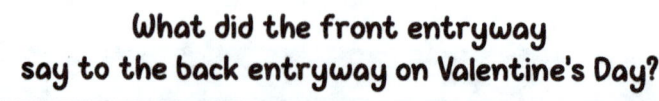

What did the front entryway say to the back entryway on Valentine's Day?

I adore you.

What did the booger say to its Valentine?

"I'm stuck on you."

Why did the paper towel not have a date for the Valentine's Dance?

He was self-absorbed.

What did the candy cane say to its girlfriend?

"You're the sweetest I know."

Why did the guitar fall in love?

Someone struck the right chord.

What did one shoe say to the other?"

"Let's be sole mates."

Why did the robot
marry his fiancée?

He couldn't resistor.

What happened when the carpet fell in love
with the self-absorbed girl?

It got walked on.

What did the paper whisper to
the other sheet of paper as the pen got near?

"I think I've finally met Mr. Write."

What did the lampshade
say to the lightbulb on Valentine's Day?

"You brighten my life."

Where are dating apps
stored on the computer?

The heart drive.

What did the glasses
say to the nose?

"I have my eyes on you."

What did the sun
say to the moon?

"I radiate for you."

What type of music terrifies
Valentine's Day balloons?

Pop.

What did the bowling ball
say to the bowling pin on Valentine's Day?

"You're right up my alley."

What did the pen
say to the paper?

"I dot my I's on you."

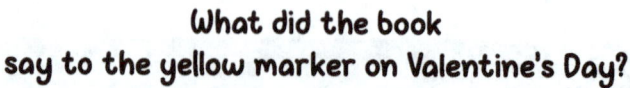

**What did the book
say to the yellow marker on Valentine's Day?**

"You are the highlight of my life."

**Why was the broom
so popular on Valentine's Day?**

It swept everyone off their feet!

**How did the planet Mars know Saturn
was giving a serious proposal?**

Saturn had a ring.

**Why did the pencil ask the sharpener
to go on a Valentine's Day adventure?**

It was having a dull day.

**What did the oil well
say to its Valentine?**

"Oil I'll ever need is you."

**How did the relationship
between the fonts work out?**

They weren't each other's type.

What did the tie
say to the shirt?

"We suit each other!"

What happened
when the two seatbelts met?

They clicked.

What did the paperclip
say to the magnet?

"I'm attracted to you."

What did the mirror
say to its Valentine?

"I can always see myself with you!"

Why didn't the bike
go to the Valentine's Day dance?

It was too tired.

What did the ruler
say to the notebook?

"You measure up to everything I need!"

What did the teapot
say to its Valentine?

"You're my cup of tea!"

Why did the skeleton
go to the Valentine's dance alone?

Because he had no body to go with!

**What did the printer
say to the laptop on Valentine's Day?**

"We've got a strong connection."

**What did one piece of dung
in the field say to the other?**

"Aren't you a cutie-poo."

Is the calendar popular
on Valentine's Day?

Yes, she has many dates.

What did the shovel
say to the dirt?

"I dig you!"

What did the dirt
say to the shovel?

"You make me hole."

What did the Earth
say to the sun on Valentine's Day?

"You're looking hot."

What did the scalp
say to the hair on Valentine's Day?

"You're growing on me."

How did the computer mice
get along on Valentine's Day?

They clicked.

**What did the volcano
say to its Valentine?**

"You look lava-ly."

**When did the car flirt
with the traffic signal?**

When it got the green light.

FRIENDS AND FAMILY

Why should a boy never kiss
his girlfriend on January 1?

It's only the first date.

Why was the girl
so excited to marry the author?

He was Mr. Write.

What do you
and I have in common?

Both are vowels.

What's the problem
with having a girlfriend who is losing weight?

You'll see less and less of her.

Why did the man fall in love
with the zoo worker?

He knew she was a keeper.

**What does a firefighter
call an ex-Valentine?**

"An old flame."

**Why is Valentine's Day
on February 14?**

Because that's the big 1-4, speaking of which, will you be the 1-4 me?

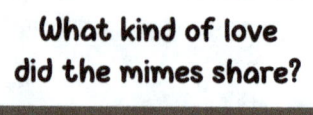

What kind of love
did the mimes share?

Unspoken.

How can you tell
if your optician is in love with you?

By the way that she looks into your eyes.

What happened when the knot-sewer
couldn't tell if his girlfriend loved him or his work?

He walked around muttering, "She loves me; she loves me knot.
She loves me; she loves me knot."

Why did the pirate bring his former girlfriend
to mark the spot where he had buried the treasure?

Because ex marks the spot.

Why did the girl bring eyeliner
to her boyfriend's home after an argument?

She wanted to make-up there.

**What did the mermaid
say to the fisherman on Valentine's Day?**

"You hooked me."

**What did the archaeologist
say to his girlfriend?**

"What do you think of my dating technique?"

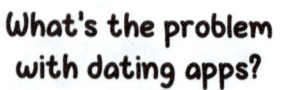

What's the problem with dating apps?

Nothing; I just prefer to date humans.

Why was the King of Hearts so in love with the Queen of Hearts?

They were suited for each other.

What did the Earthling girl say to her Martian Valentine?

"You're out of this world."

What happened when the sprinters met?

They became fast friends.

What happened when the researcher met the other researcher in the library?

It was love at first cite.

Did you hear what happened to the two construction workers who met on the job?

It was love at first site for them too.

What did the doctor reply when his girlfriend
said he had touched too many women's hearts?

"That's what heart surgeons do."

What did the maiden
say to the pirate with lady?

"You're the one eye, love."

What happened when the romantic couple went to the costume party dressed as the numeral ten?

Everyone knew she was the one for him.

What kind of love notes do mechanics write?

Heart-wrenching.

What did the musician whisper to his girlfriend on Valentine's Day?

"I love you beyond measure."

What did the carpenter say to his girlfriend?

"Wood you be my girlfriend?"

Did you hear about the geometry teachers who dated?

They were acute couple.

What did the electrician and his Valentine do?

They made sparks fly.

**Why should you
never date a cashier?**

They are always after your money.

**What did the seamstress
say to her Valentine?**

"I'm sew into you."

How did the garbageman tell his old girlfriend that he had a new girlfriend?

He dumped her.

What happened when the girl accidentally poked her boyfriend's eyes?

He stopped seeing her for a while.

Why were people surprised when the girl took the Invisible Man to the Valentine's Dance?

They didn't see what she saw in him.

Why did the patient fall in love with his cardiologist?

She touched his heart.

What did the fisherman say to his girlfriend?

"You're reel cute."

What does a girl call her rich boyfriend?

Finance

What did the pirate say to his sweetheart on Valentine's Day?

"You arrrr me hearty."

Why did the woman turn down the Renaissance actor?

She didn't like Middle Aged men.

What's it like to
see your former girlfriend?

It's ex-sighting.

Why is 12:59 p.m. considered quality time
with your Valentine?

It is one-to-one.

How did the seamstress describe
her relationship with the tailor?

"Sew-sew."

How did the man
say his long-distance relationship was going?

"So far, so good."

What's the problem
with dating a historian?

They keep remembering the past.

What do you call a priest and a nun who give up
eating on February 14 in honor of St. Valentine?

Fast friends.

What did the alien
say to his Valentine?

"You're out of this world!"

What happened when the girl didn't show up
at the track to run with her boyfriend?

He could tell they weren't going to work out.

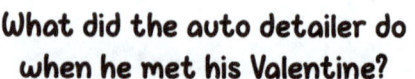

What did the auto detailer do
when he met his Valentine?

Took a shine to her.

What shape is a kiss?

Elliptical (A lip tickle).

What profession is not choosy about
who it takes to the Valentine's dance?

Archeologists will date any ol' thing.

Why did the captain insist that his Valentine
stay in his boat and not go in another boat?

He didn't want them to drift apart.

The two buddies who shared fashion secret denied being
Valentines; what did they want to be known as?

Clothes friends.

Why did the fisherman and his wife
go fishing at least once per month?

They had reel love.

**Why did the man steal
an oblong Chinese cooking pan from the beach?**

He liked taking long woks on the beach.

**If you receive an email promising you lots of Valentine's,
why shouldn't you open it?**

It's clique bait.

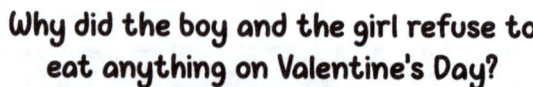

Why did the boy and the girl refuse to
eat anything on Valentine's Day?

They wanted to be fast friends.

Why did the girl fall in love
with the Martian?

He was down to earth.

Why did the boy fall in love
with the space alien?

She was out of this world.

Why did the girl drive
so slowly in her heart-shaped car?

She didn't want to experience the heart brake.

What type of road does the girl in
the heart-shaped car like to drive?

The bypass.

Why did the computer tech say he wanted
his Valentine and himself to be just like the keyboard?

"Because 'U' and 'I' are together."

Why did the music teacher
love Valentine's Day?

She had perfect harmony with her partner!

Why did the fisherman
send his crush a card?

He was angling for her heart!

Which high school teacher craves
the Valentine he had last year?

The algebra teacher is always looking for his x.

Why did the science student ask out the girl
whose locker was across from his?

They had chemistry together!

How do boy-crazy girls laugh?

"He. He. He."

Why are soccer goalies
worth pursuing?

They're keepers.

What type of relationship do you have
when a tall person dates a short person?

A long-distance relationship.

What did the teenager say when the father of the girl he was
taking to the dance stated, "I want her home by midnight"?

"You already own her home, sir."

What did the bread-maker say to his Valentine?

"I'll meet all of your kneads."

How did the chef impress the cook?

He whisked her off her feet.

What attracted the teacher
to the school janitor?

He swept her off her feet.

What did the boy do when his girlfriend was on the third floor,
and he was on the first floor, standing by a broken elevator?

He stopped and staired.

Why did the boy
call his girlfriend his "Universal Remote"?

Because she changed everything in his world for the better.

What did the geologist
say to his girlfriend?

"You're a real gem."

What did the heart surgeon
say to his Valentine?

"Aorta tell you, I want you to be my Valentine."

Why don't more parents trust matadors
around their daughters?

There's a big red flag associated with them.

**What did the airline pilot
say to his girlfriend, the stewardess?**

"You're plane awesome."

**Why didn't the baker
have a girlfriend?**

He was too kneady.

Why did the girl think her soldier boyfriend was keeping secrets from her when she asked him his rank in the army?

Because he said, "It's private."

What did the best friend say on Valentine's Day?

"You'll always be my pal-entines!"

What happened when the Invisible Man broke up with his girlfriend?

She didn't see him anymore.

Why do many tennis players remain single?

Love means nothing to them.

What did the librarian say to her Valentine?

"I'm checking you out!"

Why didn't the paranoid man refuse Valentine's flowers from the government?

He thought they were a plant from the FBI.

What did the Mars-bound astronaut
say to his girlfriend?

"I'm over the moon for you?"

What did the astronomer
say to his girlfriend?

"You are my whole universe."

What should you do if you realize there is no perfect match for you?

Begin to search for the perfect lighter.

Why do teachers make great Valentines?

They have class.

Why did the sports fan buy his girlfriend a ticket to the baseball game?

She asked to see a diamond.

What did the gardener promise his Valentine?

Good thymes.

What was the math teacher's favorite equation?

"You + Me = Valentines".

When told, "I'd like nothing better than a diamond," what did the boy buy his girlfriend?

Nothing (and he was surprised she got upset).

INTERNET CAFE

How did the boy fall in love
with the girl at the Internet café?

They clicked from the start.

What did the girl
say to her boyfriend on the moon?

"You are out of this world."

What did the fisherman
say to his Valentine?

"You're a real catch!"

Why did the student
give his teacher a Valentine?

She had class.

CHAPTER THREE:
KNOCK-KNOCK..
WHO LOVES YOU?

Valentine's Day is full of surprises, and some of the best ones come right to your door. Cards arrive in envelopes, treats get passed around, and friendly smiles seem to pop up everywhere. That makes this chapter extra special, because these jokes start the same way. With a knock.

Knock knock jokes are all about sharing. One person knocks, another answers, and before you know it, everyone wants to join in. They are easy to tell, fun to act out, and perfect for laughing together.

Inside this chapter, you will find Valentine knock knock jokes about hearts, candy, Cupid, and lots of silly surprises. Each one is like a little visitor bringing a smile with it.

So get ready to knock, listen closely, and open the door to some big laughs. The fun is waiting on the other side.

Knock-Knock.
Who's there?
Miss Singh.
Miss Singh, who?
Miss Singh (missing), you on Valentine's Day
if you won't be my Valentine.

Knock-Knock.
Who's there?
Aloe.
Aloe who?
Aloe you very much.

Knock-Knock.
Who's there?
Eye Dew.
Eye Dew who?
"Eye Dew" is what people say
when they get married.

Knock-Knock.
Who's there?
Howell.
Howell who?
Howell you get your Valentine's attention?

Knock-Knock.
Who's there?
Quick Kiss.
Quick Kiss, who?
Quick Kiss way to make good grades: study.

Knock-Knock.
Who's there?
Love Lee.
Love Lee who?
Love Lee day for a walk, don't you think?

Knock-Knock.
Who's there?
Pearl Nicholas.
Pearl Nicholas, who?
Pearl Nicholas and other jewelry are popular with
lots of women on Valentine's Day.

Knock-Knock.
Who's there?
I, Malone.
I, Malone, who?
I, Malone, right now,
so we could hang out together if you want.

Knock-Knock.
Who's there?
Mel.
Mel who?
Mel your Valentine's early to make sure
they arrive on time.

Knock-Knock.
Who's there?
I.M.N. Love.
I.M.N. Love who?
I.M.N. Love with you, that's who.

Knock-Knock.
Who's there?
Cindy.
Cindy who?
Cindy Valentine's Day cards a couple of days early.

Knock-Knock.
Who's there?
Pooch.
Pooch who?
Pooch your hand in mine.

Knock-Knock.
Who's there?
Bo.
Bo who?
Bo and arrow are something Cupid carries.

Knock-Knock.
Who's there?
Mei Ling.
Mei Ling who?
Mei Ling, your Valentine's cards early is smart.

Knock-Knock.
Who's there?
Blueberry.
Blueberry who?
Blueberry hard, but I couldn't blow out the candles after the romantic meal.

Knock-Knock.
Who's there?
Gorilla Dreams.
Gorilla Dreams, who?
Gorilla Dreams (girl of my dreams),
will you be my Valentine?

Knock-Knock.
Who's there?
Howie DeWinn.
Howie DeWinn, who?
Howie DeWinn? Have you got a smile on your face?

Knock-Knock.
Who's there?
Candle.
Candle who?
Candle people be as funny as you are?

Knock-Knock.
Who's there?
Wifi.
Wifi who?
Wifi love you.

Knock-Knock.
Who's there?
Wanda B.
Wanda B., who?
Wanda B. your Valentine.

Knock-Knock.
Who's there?
Rome Antics.
Roman Antics, who?
Roman Antics find love wherever they go.

Knock-Knock.
Who's there?
Toby.
Toby who?
Toby your Valentine
would be lots of fun.

Knock-Knock.
Who's there?
Tammi.
Tammi who?
Tammi you love me.

Knock-Knock.
Who's there?
Lovette.
Lovette who?
Lovette or leave it.

Knock-Knock.
Who's there?
Roman Ticks.
Roman Ticks, who?
Roman Ticks tend to be optimistic
and to find love and goodness everywhere.

Knock-Knock.
Who's there?
Chuck.
Chuck who?
Chuck-olate is a very popular candy
on Valentine's Day.

Knock-Knock.
Who's there?
Love.
Love who?
Love you.

Knock-Knock.
Who's there?
Seymour fellows.
Seymour fellows who?
**Seymour fellows and you will likely
meet a handsome one.**

Knock-Knock.
Who's there?
Ray Zen.
Ray Zen, who?
**Ray Zen to the store to get you
a Valentine's Day card.**

Knock-Knock.
Who's there?
Sue Render.
Sue Render, who?
Sue Render to love this Valentine's Day.

Knock-Knock.
Who's there?
With . . . Achoo.
With . . . Achoo, who?
With . . . Achoo, life is not as fun.

Knock-Knock.
Who's there?
Sadie.
Sadie who?
Sadie words, "Be my Valentine,"
and I'll be your Valentine.

Knock-Knock.
Who's there?
Rose.
Rose who?
Rows the boat to the dock
to pick up his sweetheart.

Knock-Knock.
Who's there?
Baby Owl.
Baby Owl who?
Baby Owl gladly be your Valentine.

Knock-Knock.
Who's there?
Sweden.
Sweden who?
Sweden chocolaty is how I like my candy.

Knock-Knock.
Who's there?
A Door.
A Door who?
A Door you, Valentine.

Knock-Knock.
Who's there?
Just Passion.
Just Passion, who?
**Just Passion, and I thought I'd stop
to say hello to you.**

Knock-Knock.
Who's there?
Willie.
Willie who?
Willie want to be your Valentine?

Knock-Knock.
Who's there?
Roman Sing.
Roman Sing, who?
**Roman Sing can be done with cards, flowers, candy,
songs, and numerous other ways.**

Knock-Knock.
Who's there?
Wan Chu.
Wan Chu, who?
Wan Chu to be my Valentine.

Knock-Knock.
Who's there?
Handsome.
Handsome who?
Handsome Valentine's candy to me, please.

Knock-Knock.
Who's there?
Marie Mee.
Marie Mee, who?
Marie Mee and we will be husband and wife.

Knock-Knock.
Who's there?
Alligator.
Alligator who?
Alligator (all I get her) for Valentine's Day was a card;
I hope she's okay with that.

Knock-Knock.
Who's there?
Aiken Hart.
Aiken Hart, who?
Aiken Hart is something nobody
wants on Valentine's Day.

Knock-Knock.
Who's there?
Mallet.
Mallet who?
Mallet by putting it in the mailbox; let the post
office deliver your Valentine's card to your
sweetheart for you.

Knock-Knock.
Who's there?
Tammy Youloveme.
Tammy Youloveme who?
Tammy Youloveme, I want
to be your Valentine.

Knock-Knock.
Who's there?
Roman Antique.
Roman Antique who?
Roman Antique evening awaits you
if you'll be my Valentine.

Knock-Knock.
Who's there?
Marius Quick.
Marius Quick, who?
Marius Quick (marry us quick)
is a request the pastor often hears.

Knock-Knock.
Who's there?
A Tractor.
A Tractor who?
A Tractor, if you want her
for your Valentine.

Knock-Knock.
Who's there?
Bot.
Bot who?
Bot you some flowers.

Knock-Knock.
Who's there?
Candice B.
Candice B., who?
Candice B love?

Knock-Knock.
Who's there?
Wilbur Wright.
Wilbur Wright who?
Wilbur Wright back with more
Valentine's jokes.

Knock-Knock.
Who's there?
french Ship.
french Ship who?
french Ship and love are what
Valentine's Day is all about.

Knock-Knock.
Who's there?
Gladyse C. Hugh.
Gladyse C. Hugh who?
Gladyse C. Hugh, do you
want to be my Valentine?

Knock-Knock.
Who's there?
Tommy.
Tommy who?
Tommy the stories of Cupid; I'll listen.

Knock-Knock.
Who's there?
Aisle B.
Aisle B. who?
Aisle B your Valentine.

Knock-Knock.
Who's there?
Phyliss Guyin.
Phyliss Guyin who?
Phyliss Guyin (fill this guy in), what are your plans for Valentine's Day?

Knock-Knock.
Who's there?
Will U.
Will U. who?
Will U. be my Valentine?

Knock-Knock.
Who's there?
Candice Day.
Candice who?
Candice Day get any better?

Knock-Knock.
Who's there?
Oliver.
Oliver who?
Oliver friends want to be her Valentine.

Knock-Knock.
Who's there?
Noah Scape.
Noah Scape who?
Noah Scape from this crazy Valentine humor.

Knock-Knock.
Who's there?
Norma Leigh.
Norma Leigh who?
**Norma Leigh I mail
my Valentine's Day cards a week early.**

Knock-Knock.
Who's there?
Arthur.
Arthur who?
Arthur any Valentine's in the mailbox yet?

Knock-Knock.

Who's there?

Howard.

Howard who?

Howard you like to be my Valentine?

Knock-Knock.

Who's there?

Believing.

Believing who?

Believing flowers, candy, and a copy
of this book for my Valentine.

DID YOU ENJOY THE BOOK?

If you did, we are ecstatic. If not, please write your complaint to us and we will ensure we fix it.

If you're feeling generous, there is something important that you can help me with – tell other people that you enjoyed the book.

Ask a grown-up to write about it on Amazon. When they do, more people will find out about the book. It also lets Amazon know that we are making kids around the world laugh. Even a few words and ratings would go a long way.

If you have any ideas or jokes that you think are super funny, please let us know. We would love to hear from you. Our email address is -

riddleland@riddlelandforkids.com

ABOUT RIDDLELAND

Riddleland is a mum + dad run publishing company. We are passionate about creating fun and innovative books to help children develop their reading skills and fall in love with reading. If you have suggestions for us or want to work with us, shoot us an email at riddleland@riddlelandforkids.com Our family's favorite quote:

"Creativity is an area in which younger people have a tremendous advantage since they have an endearing habit of always questioning past wisdom and authority."

~ Bill Hewlett

www.ingramcontent.com/pod-product-compliance
Lightning Source LLC
Chambersburg PA
CBHW061656120626
46550CB00003B/958